The Piano
and other keyboard instruments

Rita Storey

A+

Smart Apple Media

Smart Apple Media
P.O. Box 3263, Mankato, Minnesota 56002

Printed in the United States of America at Corporate Graphics in North Mankato, Minnesota

Published by arrangement with the Watts Publishing Group Ltd, London.

Art director: Jonathan Hair
Series designed and created for Franklin Watts by Painted Fish Ltd.
Designer: Rita Storey
Editor: Fiona Corbridge
Adviser: Helen MacGregor

Picture credits
istockphoto.com pp. 4, 5, 7, 12, 16, 17, 20, 21, 22, 23, 24, 25; Robin Little/Redferns
p. 26; Tudor Photography pp. 3, 6, 8, 9, 10, 11, 13, 14, 18, 19;
Ulster Orchestra p. 15.

Cover images: Tudor Photography, Banbury (top); istock.com (bottom left,
middle and right)

All photos posed by models.
Thanks to Husnen Ahmad, Hannah Barton, and Maddi Indun

Library of Congress Cataloging-in-Publication Data

Storey, Rita.
  The piano and other keyboard instruments / Rita Storey.
     p. cm. -- (Let's make music)
  Includes bibliographical references and index.
  Summary: "Introduces the piano and keyboard instruments while discussing
how to read music; also looks at different ways of producing music using a
keyboard instrument"--Provided by publisher.
  ISBN 978-1-59920-215-0 (hardcover)
 1. Piano--Juvenile literature. 2. Keyboard instruments--Juvenile literature. I.
Title.
  ML549.S76 2010
  786--dc22
                        2008040714

022310
1204

Contents

The Piano   6

The Sound   8

The Keys   10

Chords and Scales   12

Upright or Grand?   14

Playing Together   16

Electronic Keyboard   18

Computer Music   20

Pipe Organ   22

Other Keyboards   24

Key Notes   26

Listen!   27

Glossary   29

Index   30

Words in **bold** are in the glossary.

The Piano

The piano is a musical instrument. You sit down and use both hands to play it.

Pianos usually have eighty-eight **keys**. Some of these are white and some are black.

The body of a piano is called the case. The keys in modern pianos are made of wood and plastic.

This girl is playing a piano.

Making a Sound

To make a sound on a piano, press the keys with your fingers.

Different Sounds

Each key makes a different sound, or musical note. You can press them one by one or several together.

Listen!
Pages 27 and 28 tell you about music played on keyboard instruments that you can listen to.

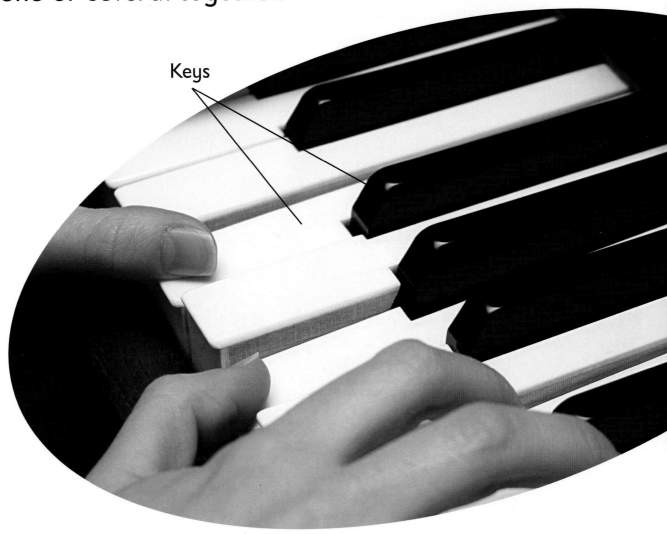

Keys

7

The Sound

When you press a piano key, it makes a tiny hammer hit a metal string inside the piano. The string begins to wobble very fast—it is vibrating.

Sound Waves

When the string **vibrates**, it makes the air around it move as well. The way that the air moves is called a **sound wave**.

Louder

The sound waves bounce around inside the piano and make the sounds louder.

Pressing the keys moves the hammers inside a piano.

Stopping the Sound

When you take your fingers off the keys, pads stop the strings from vibrating. These pads are called dampers.

Tuning

To make each string play the correct note, a piano has to be tuned. This is done by turning the tuning pins.

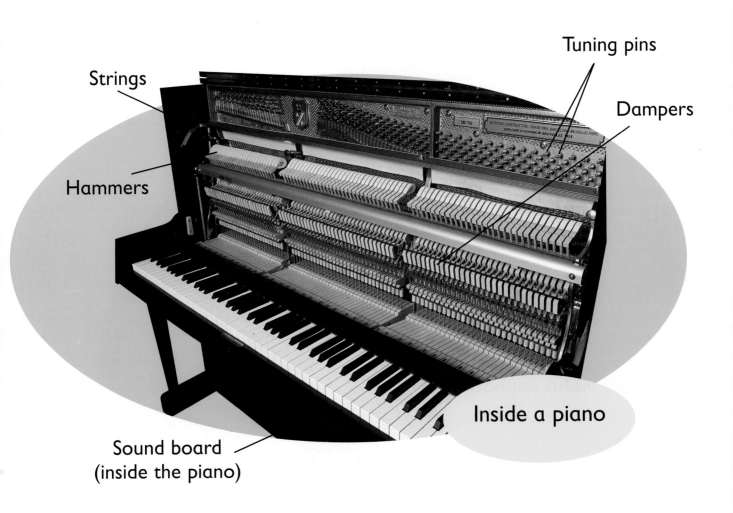

Tuning pins

Strings

Dampers

Hammers

Sound board
(inside the piano)

Inside a piano

The Keys

Each key on a piano makes a different sound. You can press several keys together to make lots of different sounds.

High and Low

Some musical notes are high and some are low. We call this their **pitch**.

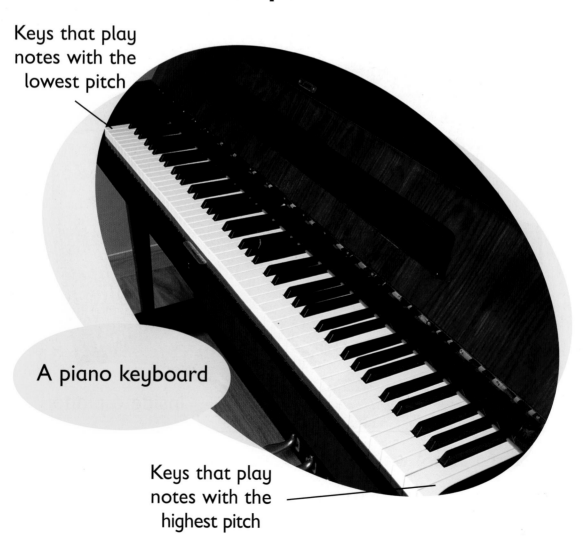

Keys that play notes with the lowest pitch

A piano keyboard

Keys that play notes with the highest pitch

Keyboard

The line of keys on a piano is called a keyboard. The sound that each key plays goes from low pitch at one end of the keyboard to high pitch at the other end.

Playing Notes

To make quieter sounds, press the keys gently. For louder sounds, press the keys harder.

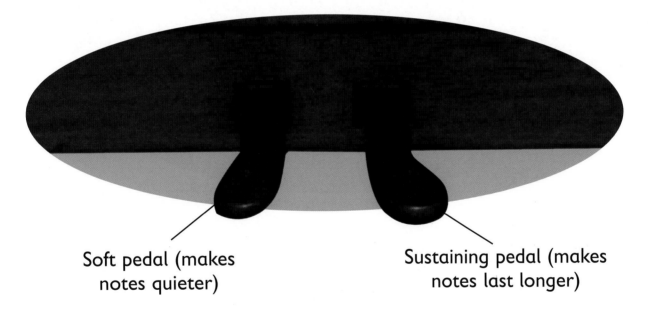

Soft pedal (makes notes quieter)

Sustaining pedal (makes notes last longer)

Pedals

There are two (or sometimes three) pedals near the floor, which you press with your feet. The one on the left makes the notes sound quieter, and the one on the right makes them last longer and seem louder.

Chords and Scales 🎵

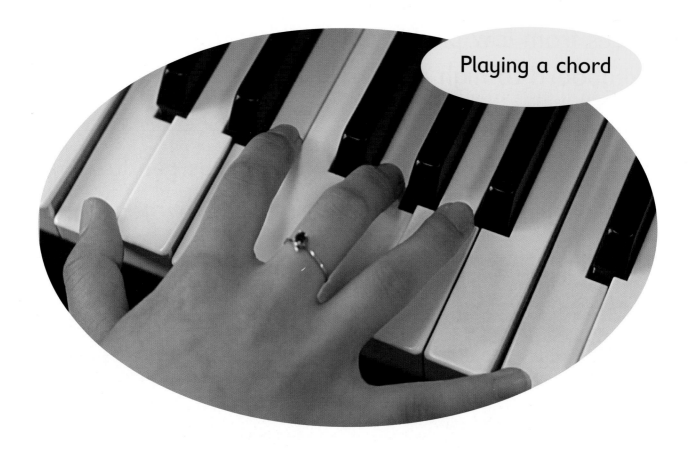

Playing a chord

There are lots of different ways to play notes on a piano. A good pianist (piano player) uses both hands and plays up to ten keys at a time.

A Chord

When two or more keys are held down together, the notes that are played are called a chord.

Black and White

The white keys on a piano keyboard play notes called **natural notes**. The black keys are grouped in twos and threes. They play notes called **sharps** and **flats**.

Music Notes

To be able to play music that other people have made up, or composed, you need to understand how to read music. Music is written in musical notes.

The notes are written on five lines called a staff. The place of a note on the staff tells us how high or low it is. This is called its pitch.

Notes are named after letters: A, B, C, D, E, F, G. **Symbols** tell us how long or short a note is. The length of the notes in a piece of music make up its **rhythm**.

A scale is a set of notes played up and then down the keyboard. A scale of eight notes is called an octave. The octave shown here goes from one C on the keyboard to the next C. The notes are natural notes.

C D E F G A B C

These keys play sharps and flats.

These keys play natural notes.

13

Upright or Grand?

There are two kinds of pianos—an upright piano and a grand piano.

Upright Pianos

Most people who have a piano have an upright piano. It is sometimes called an acoustic piano.

An upright (or acoustic) piano

A grand piano being played in an orchestra.

Grand Pianos

Grand pianos are used in **orchestras** and played by pianists giving a **concert**.

The strings in a grand piano are laid flat, going away from the keyboard. A grand piano is larger than an upright piano but has the same number of keys.

There is a smaller type of grand piano called a baby grand.

Playing Together

There are lots of different ways that a piano can be used.

Play Along

The piano is often played to **accompany** singers and other **solo** instruments.

Singers may use a piano to help them sing notes at the correct pitch when they are practicing or performing.

This pianist is accompanying a violinist as she practices.

Duets

Sometimes two people play a piano together. This is called a duet.

These performers are playing a duet.

Trios and Quartets

A piano may be played with a small group of other instruments. A piano trio has a piano, a violin, and a cello.

In a piano quartet, there are four instruments—a piano, a violin, a viola, and a cello.

Electronic Keyboard

On an electronic keyboard, you play the keys in the same way as on a piano. The keyboard must be plugged in to make it work.

When you press a key, the sound is produced **electronically**.

Playing an electronic keyboard

Rhythms

The keyboard can play different rhythms and beats in the background as you play the keys. It can also be made to sound like other instruments.

Light Keyboards

Keyboards that you use at home or at school usually have fewer than eighty-eight keys. They are easy to carry from place to place.

Music Notes

Beat and Rhythm

All music has a beat. This is a regular sound, rather like the ticking of a clock. The beat can be fast or slow. It is the heartbeat of a piece of music.

Rhythm is the pattern of sounds and silences in a piece of music.

The melody, or tune, of a piece of music makes it different from any other piece of music. This is the important part!

The controls on an electronic keyboard

19

Computer Music

This girl is playing a MIDI keyboard attached to a computer.

Many electronic keyboards can be linked to a computer.

MIDI Keyboard

A MIDI keyboard does not produce a sound when you play it. It sends a signal to a computer that changes it into music.

The sounds are passed through **amplifiers** and **loudspeakers** so they can be heard.

New Sounds

The computer can use the signals from the keyboard to do other things. It can change sounds that have been stored in the computer or produce new sounds.

It can also copy the sounds of all sorts of musical instruments.

These controls can change the sounds.

Pipe Organ

A pipe organ is a wind instrument. It makes sounds by blowing air through pipes of different sizes.

Playing a Pipe Organ

There are at least two keyboards, which you play with your hands. There are also many pedals that you play with your feet.

Organ Stops

The sound of the pipes can be changed by pulling controls called organ stops.

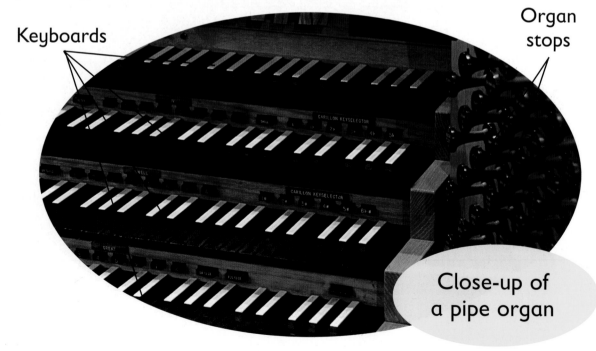

Keyboards

Organ stops

Close-up of a pipe organ

Pipes
Bellows blow air through the organ pipes, which are different sizes. The large pipes make a deep, low sound. The small pipes make a high-pitched sound.

A Big Sound
Pipe organs are very large. They are often used in buildings, such as churches, because they make a loud sound.

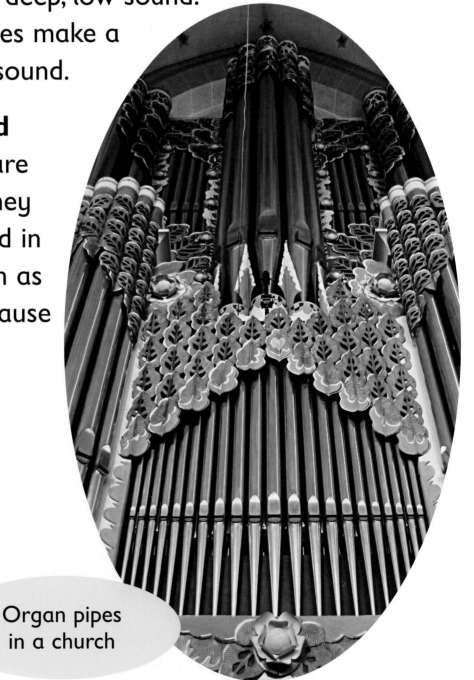

Organ pipes in a church

23

Other Keyboards

Other musical instruments also have a keyboard that you play.

Harpsichord

The harpsichord looks a bit like a piano, but sounds very different. When the player presses the keys on the keyboard, small hooks pluck the strings.

Harmonium
The harmonium is a type of organ. It is often used to play Indian music.

Electric Organ
An electric organ is smaller than a pipe organ and does not have pipes.

Accordion
The accordion is played by using a keyboard and a set of buttons. You have to squeeze a set of bellows in and out as you play, and the air from this makes the sound.

Key Notes

Keyboard instruments can be used to play many different styles of music.

Jazz

Jazz is a style of music that began in New Orleans, USA. The sound of the piano is an important part of jazz music.

Pop and Rock

Pop and rock musicians use electronic keyboards and computers to make new and exciting sounds.

This band is making music using electronic keyboards.

Listen!

Web Sites

Play along with a virtual piano! Learn about melodies and how songwriters use melodies as a foundation to create new works of music. Also hear how a melody can sound fresh and new when played with a different rhythm or instrument at:
http://www.pbs.org/jazz/lounge/lab_virtual_piano.htm

Practice your scales and learn the names of the notes using a flash player. Hit each key with a click of your mouse and hear what the note would sound like on a piano. Press another key to hear the piano play a tune at:
http://numbera.com/musictheory/piano.aspx

View an interactive map of a pipe organ. Click on the icons to hear what a real pipe organ sounds like! Use the translator to find out what different parts of the pipe organ are called in different languages at:
http://www.pipe-organs.net

Play "Be a Rockin' Rhythm Master!" and other cool games. Compose your own music and even go back in time using the Composer Time Machine. Test your memory with the Note Name Game at:
http://www.classicsforkids.com/games/

Have you ever wondered what a piano tuner sees when he or she opens up a piano? Look at neat pictures of the inside of different pianos. View all the different parts of the piano and see how they fit together at:
http://www.lipmanpianos.com/inside.html

CDs

Piano
Wolfgang Amadeus Mozart: *Variations on "Ah, vous dirai-je, Maman"* (Twinkle, Twinkle, Little Star).
Ludwig van Beethoven: *Für Elise*; Piano Sonatas
Camille Saint-Saëns: *Carnival of the Animals*
Scott Joplin: *Piano Rags*
Dave Brubeck: *Take Five*
Sparky's Magic Piano.
Robert Schumann: *Scenes of Childhood*
Frederic Chopin: Mazurkas and Waltzes
Claude Debussy: *Children's Corner*
Percy Grainger: *English Country Garden*
Eric Satie: *Gymnopedies*
Duke Ellington: *C Jam Blues*
Steve Reich: *Six Pianos*

Organ
Johann Sebastian Bach: Preludes and Fugues
Camille Saint-Saëns: *Symphony No. 3 for Organ and Orchestra*

Harpsichord
Domenico Scarlatti: Sonatas
The Fitzwilliam Virginal Book

Accordion
French Café Accordion Music
Histoire du Tango

Glossary

Accompany To play an instrument to support a singer or musician as he or she performs.

Amplifier Equipment for increasing the strength of a sound.

Bellows A device for making a strong flow of air.

Concert A public musical performance by singers or musicians.

Electronic, electronically Powering devices using electricity.

Flat A musical note that is pitched slightly lower than the natural note of the same letter (e.g. G flat is lower than G).

Key A lever on an instrument that you press down to play.

Loudspeaker A device for changing electrical signals into sounds that we can hear.

Natural notes Notes that are not sharp or flat. On the piano, they are the white keys.

Orchestra A large group of performers playing various musical instruments.

Pitch A high musical note or sound is said to have a high pitch. A low musical note or sound is said to have a low pitch.

Rhythm The regular pattern of sound in music.

Sharp A musical note that is pitched slightly higher than the natural note of the same letter (e.g. G sharp is higher than G).

Solo Playing alone.

Sound wave A wave that transmits sound through the air.

Symbol A shape used to represent something else.

Vibrate; vibration Moving back and forth rapidly.

Index

accompanying   16
accordions   25
amplifiers   20

beat   19
bellows   23, 25

chords   12, 27
composers   21
computer music
   20–21, 26
concerts   15

duets   17

electric organs
   25
electronic
   keyboards
   18–19, 20–21, 26

flats   13

grand pianos   15

harmoniums   24

harpsichords   24

jazz   26

keyboards   10–11,
   22, 24–25
keys   6, 10–11, 13

loudspeakers   20

manuals   23
melodies   19
MIDI keyboards
   20
music   13, 26,
   27–28

natural notes   13

octaves   13
orchestras   15, 27
organ stops   22

pedals   11, 22
piano quartets
   17

piano trios   17
pianos   6–7, 8–9,
   10–11, 12–13,
   14–15, 16–17
pipe organs
   22–23, 27
pitch   10, 13
playing notes   7,
   11, 12

rhythm   13, 19

scales   13, 27
sharps   13
sound waves   8–9
symbols   13

tuning   9

upright pianos   14

vibration   8